my soul pages

my soul pages
A Companion to Writing Down Your Soul

JANET CONNER

Mango Publishing
CORAL GABLES

Cover Design: Jim Warner
Cover Photo/illustration: adapted from Tamas Galambos's "Blue Owl," from Private Collection /
The Bridgeman Art Library, © the artist.
Layout & Design: Nancy Condon

For permission requests, please contact the publisher at:
Mango Publishing Group
2850 S Douglas Road, 2nd Floor
Coral Gables, FL 33134 USA
info@mango.bz

For special orders, quantity sales, course adoptions and corporate sales, please email the
publisher at sales@mango.bz. For trade and wholesale sales, please contact Ingram Publisher
Services at customer.service@ingramcontent.com or +1.800.509.4887.

My Soul Pages: *A Companion to Writing Down Your Soul*

Library of Congress Cataloging-in-Publication data is available upon request.
ISBN: (print) 978-1-57324-496-1,
BISAC category code: OCC019000, BODY, MIND & SPIRIT / Inspiration & Personal Growth

Printed in the United States of America

Acknowledgments

I am oh so grateful to Daniel Ladinsky for encouraging me to become best friends with Hafiz, and for granting permission to quote excerpts from his heart-soaring translations of Hafiz in *The Gift, The Subject Tonight Is Love,* and *I Heard God Laughing,* as well as wisdom from other mystical poets in *Love Poems from God.* Thank you to Nancy Barton for whispering words of wisdom and joy in my ear, miraculously, always at the perfect moment. And to Jan Johnson, publisher of Conari Press, who spread her special grace upon this project and brought it to life. And to my Voice, my beautiful Voice, words pale. Thank you for holding my hand as you spoke, and continue to speak to me still, encouraging me to "use words to connect people to the Light."

When you begin writing down your soul, you activate a continuous loop of communication between you and the wise Voice within. You write, and the Voice listens; the Voice writes, and you listen. It's that simple—and that mysterious. The Möbius strip is a perfect symbol of this "conversation that never ends," because the strip has no beginning and no end.

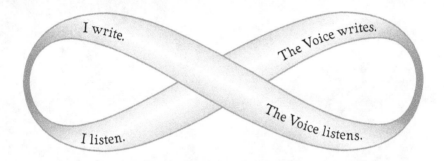

You may find it helpful to write your Voice's name on this Möbius strip. For example, if your Voice is known to you as "Grace," write Grace on the two blank lines. If this image speaks to you, consider tracing your finger over it before you write, saying aloud: "I write. _____ listens. _____ writes. I listen." Slowly speaking these four short sentences as you meditatively run your finger over the strip can be a lovely, easy way to set your intention to connect with your Voice.

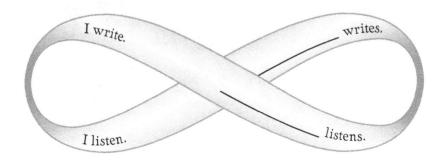

Möbius strip art by Sandy Cromp|DCDeziner

The Lute Will Beg

You need to become a pen
in the Sun's hand.

We need for the earth to sing
through our pores and our eyes.

The body will again become restless
until your soul paints all its beauty
upon the sky.

Don't tell me, dear ones,
that what Hafiz says is not true,

for when the heart tastes its glorious destiny
and you awake to our constant need
for your love

God's lute will beg
for your
hands.

—Hafiz, from *The Gift* by Daniel Ladinsky

Welcome My Beloved,

I am so glad we are here, hand-in-hand. From the beginning I have been with you. I am always with you. And you, Beloved, are always with me. Whether you know it or not, feel my presence or not, see me or not; I am here. Where you walk, there I am. Where you sit, I am. Where you mourn, I am. When you write, I am inside the words. When you clap your hands in joy, I am that sound. What you seek, I am. What you love, I have always loved. And what I have always loved—is you. Because you are in me, and I, I am in you. Tell me now, Precious One, what is in your—our—heart.

The Voice

A note from the author

The first time I scrawled "Dear God" across the top of a page, I was deep in crisis. I had no real concept of what I was doing; I just threw myself onto the page, filling ten, twenty, sometimes thirty angry pages a day. As my pen raced across the paper, I made an astonishing discovery: I could spill my heart, beg for help, and guidance would appear. Mind you, I didn't always like what I saw. For months, I wrestled with the Voice, screaming, "That's NOT what I want!" But eventually, I threw my hands up and started living my guidance. Once I did, everything changed, and now it is my great joy to share this sweet, easy way to access the limitless well of divine guidance available in each and every one of us.

I am delighted this *Writing Down Your Soul* companion is *now* in your hands. It is a journal—and more. If you are unfamiliar with the seven steps to get into the theta brain wave state, please take a moment to review them; they are on the next page. Incorporating these simple actions into your writing practice will help you get out of your bangling, wrangling conscious mind and into that sweet spot where the Voice resides. The writing pages are lined on the right side and blank on the left. Use the two sides any way you like. Here's what I do: I write my daily dialogue on the right side and capture the Voice's blessings and guidance on the left. As you turn the pages, you will be greeted by excerpts from *Writing Down Your Soul*, heart-soaring lines from my favorite mystical poets, and quotes directly from the Voice. Some of the Voice's words appeared on my own journal pages, but most came from soul writers just like you.

Meister Eckhart described writing down your soul perfectly:

"They can be a great help—words.
They can become the spirit's hands and lift and caress you."
—*Love Poems from God*, by Daniel Ladinsky

So be lifted. Be caressed. Know that when you pick up a pen, whether you are angry or peaceful, sad or joyful, afraid or grateful, or anywhere in between, the Voice is there. As the conversation unfolds, you will discover someone else, someone very special—your whole, authentic, holy self. Be blessed, my friend, and enjoy the conversation.

Janet Conner / Ozona, Florida / January 11, 2011

What Happens When You Write Down Your Soul?

You exit conscious mind and enter the theta brain wave state.

As you open and release your story onto the page, you get in touch with your authentic self—your very soul.

As you connect with and activate the Voice of wisdom within, you ask for and receive the guidance and direction you need to live the life you are here to live.

Seven Steps to Get into the Theta Brain Wave State:

1. Quantum physics clearly demonstrates that the universe is run on intention. Take advantage of that truth, and begin soul writing by setting your intention to connect with the Voice. You can do that by saying a brief blessing, running your finger over the Möbius strip on the title page, visualizing light, or holding a thought. This sounds simple (and it is simple), but don't skip over this first step. When you set your intention to go deep, you immediately elevate your writing experience.

2. Begin by writing a salutation to the Voice by name: "Dear _____ ," If you don't have a name, write "Dear Voice." As the dialogue evolves, you can ask for and receive a private and personal name. Once you have a special name, use it whenever you write—on and off the page—anytime you want to ask for help or guidance or grace.

3. Write by hand. When you look at a monitor, your eyes deliver information to your brain and you can easily get yanked back into your conscious mind. With practice, it is possible to stay in theta on the computer, but at least at the beginning, write by hand to get a feel for the presence of the Voice in your hand, your pen, and your whole body.

4. Activate all five senses. The more senses you involve, the more powerful the practice.

    - Vision is automatically engaged.

    - Touch is obviously involved.

    - If you write in silence, hearing may not appear to be engaged, but the portions of your brain responsible for hearing are firing as you write. If you wish to have theta music playing gently in the background, visit www.writingdownyoursoul.com for more information.

    - Activate your most powerful sense—the sense of smell. Light a candle, use essential oils, enjoy fresh flowers… Find your own unique way to envelop your writing space with an aroma you love.

    - To activate the sense of taste, drink water after you finish, whispering any wisdom, blessings, or messages that come through. If nothing else, say thank you.

5. Ask lots and lots of open-ended questions. Questions are the magic that activates the Voice. Let the questions come pouring through your hand without conscious thought or judgment. One question will lead to another and another and another, and you'll find yourself having a conversation with the Voice that truly surprises you.

6. Write fast. Writing quickly is a trick that helps you get ahead of all the old programs running in your head. When you want new information, deep answers to deep questions, access to real creativity or breakthrough thinking, pick up your writing speed and let the words fly. Don't bother with grammar, punctuation, legible handwriting, or logic. And sentences? Who needs sentences! Write like you talk, in bursts and phrases. One last word of wisdom, and this is important: Don't edit. Don't scratch out. Don't judge. Just go forward, forward, forward. You'll be amazed at what lies ahead.

7. Last, be grateful. Whether it was a delightful experience or not, you were heard. And that is enough. Say thank you.

Opening Blessing

I am here.

And I know you are here, too.

I am open.

My heart is open, my mind is open, my soul is open, my hand is open.

I am open.

Thank you in advance for your words and your wisdom,

your guidance and your grace.

I am so blessed. I am so blessed.

I am

so deeply blessed.

You are welcome to use this blessing as is or alter it. Or, best of all, write your own. Just ask the Voice for guidance and your own perfect blessing will emerge.

You will find who you are in your soul. It is your soul's journey, your life to enjoy.

O listen—

Listen more carefully

To what is inside of you right now.

—Hafiz, "Out of the Mouths of a Thousand Birds"

The Voice will reveal itself to you over time. Your understanding will evolve, and your trust and intimacy will grow. In the end, the Voice is who you believe it to be, where you perceive it to be, what you know it to be.

*It is only your belief that you don't know
that keeps you from knowing*

The realized soul can play with this universe
the way a child can a ball.

—Saint Theresa of Avila, "The Grail"

Deep learning requires deep listening. To listen deeply, you must open your innermost spiritual ear.

Surrender. You are not the one in control.

This place where you are right now
God circled on a map for you.

—Hafiz, "This Place Where You Are Right Now"

Things are not happening to you; they are happening for you. If you want to ask "Why is this happening to me?" ask instead, "Why did my soul call this forth?"

If you could just see the lightness of your being . . .
You are beauty itself.

I wish I could show you,

When you are lonely or in darkness,

The Astonishing Light

Of your own Being!

—Hafiz, "You Are with the Friend Now"

This is a conversation with the all-knowing, all-loving, all-listening energy that created you and loves you and will not—cannot—remove its love.

You are here to experience the expansion of the divine. Each time you are with us, we all expand and you expand; in fact, the universe expands. We are always with you. Our joy in being with you at this moment is beyond words.

Love is

the perfect stillness

and the greatest excitement, and most profound act,

and the word almost as complete

as His name.

    —Rabia, "The Perfect Stillness"

Perhaps each of us have a starved place, and each of us knows deep down what we need to fill that place. To find the courage to trust and honor the search, to follow the voice that tells us what we need to do, even when it doesn't seem to make sense, is a worthy pursuit.

—Sue Bender

It is only fear that keeps what you want from coming to you.

When you ask the Voice
for understanding, you
create space in your heart
for fresh awareness, new
learning, real discernment,
and profound seeking....
You express a willingness
to go deep to tap into the
Truth of the Universe.

Write all that worries you on
a piece of parchment;
Offer it to God.

Even from the distance of a millennium
I can lean the flame in my heart
Into your life

And turn
All that frightens you
Into holy
Incense
Ash.

—Hafiz, "Troubled"

Don't ask a soft question because you're afraid to hear the answer to a hard one. Ask what you really, really want to know. Ask for your soul's truth. If that means putting a gutsy, tough question out there, go for it. The big Voice responds in equal measure to your small voice. And the power of its answer will be in direct proportion to the energy of your question.

How do you trust? One word—decide. And if trust seems too far away today, hold onto hope. For today, hope is enough.

It's rigged—everything, in your favor. So there is nothing to worry about.

—Rumi, "It's Rigged"

The only way to reach the state of knowing is to let go of all the normal, earth-bound disbelief and step into a state of trust.

Know that you are safe. Safe and loved. Safe. And loved.
Take in these words and know that they are true.

We are people who need to love,

Because love is the soul's life,

Love is simply creation's greatest joy.

—Hafiz, "The Stairway of Existence"

Release the need to find a "right" answer. If you write with an open ear, an understanding heart, and a deep knowing that no matter what you write, you are safe and loved, the information your soul seeks will make itself known.

Do you believe that I love you? Do you believe that I will take care of you? Then trust that, and the knowing will follow.

And love says,
"I will, I will take care of you,"
To everything that is near.

— Hafiz, "And Love Says"

Be patient. You are where
you are, and where
you are is good. In fact,
you can't be any other
place. Trust the process
and know that you are
on the right path.

When in turmoil, flow on the good. There is always an answer in the good. As you contemplate the good, you raise your vibration higher and higher into the all-good. There is nothing you cannot be, do, or have by rising to the good, flowing into it. In the good there is love, appreciation, joy, and gratitude. This is the place from which all flows.

Gratitude before me,

gratitude behind me,

gratitude to the left of me,

gratitude to the right of me,

gratitude above me

gratitude below me,

gratitude within me

gratitude all around me.

—Angeles Arrien

Gratitude for the
journey—the whole
journey—changes
everything.

Forgive your mistakes. How can you condemn what I have already forgiven?

Forgiveness

Is the cash you need.

—Hafiz, "Forgiveness Is the Cash"

The Voice does not
judge. The Voice simply
listens. And there is no
greater gift than that.

Do not judge yourself or your role. Your role is to be your Self. Honor your Self as we do. Honor your truth. Honor who you are, who you are made to be, who you are becoming every day.

O God

help me

to believe

the truth about myself

no matter

how beautiful it is!

—Sister Macrina Wiederkehr,
"A Prayer to Own Your Beauty"

When you begin to identify your soul's desires and purpose, you simultaneously feel the urge to start creating an external life that mirrors your internal one. The status quo will no longer do.

Grant yourself an amnesty. Apply a peace treaty to your heart. You are no longer your own enemy.

"It is time to come to your senses. You are to live and to learn to laugh. You are to learn to listen to the cursed radio music of life and to reverence the spirit behind it and to laugh at its distortions. So there you are. More will not be asked of you."

—Herman Hesse, Steppenwolf

Your story is your healer. In every story is conflict, and within the conflict is the chance for change, for growth, for development. The value is in what the story is telling you; it is your guidance from Spirit.

I am a little pencil
in the hand of a writing God
who is sending a love letter
to the world.

—Mother Teresa

I was once spiritually ill — we all pass through that —
but one day the intelligence
in my soul
cured
me.

—Meister Eckhart, "An Insidious Idol"

As you write, you dive
below the conscious to
thoughts and feelings
you didn't know you had,
and you soar above the
conscious to experience
real understanding,
safety, and peace.

"The dictionary defines night in terms of day and day in terms of night. Can we find a way to talk about light and dark without talking about good and bad? To love both day and night? Can we hold the beauty of both in the same breath?"

—J. Ruth Gendler

Don't say, "That is impossible, that can't be done."
Become like a child. To the child all things are possible.

Writing down your soul is a layered discovery that reveals itself over time. Just give yourself to the writing, and know that when you are ready you will receive the guidance and understanding you seek.

How do geese know when to fly to the sun? Who tells them the seasons? How do we, humans, know when it's time to move on? As with the migrant birds, so surely with us, there is a voice within, if only we would listen to it, that tells us certainly when to go forth into the unknown.

—Elisabeth Kübler-Ross, *The Wheel of Life*

God
Disguised
As a myriad things and
Playing a game
Of tag

Has kissed you and said,
"You're it—
I mean, you're Really IT!"

Now
It does not matter
What you believe or feel
For something wonderful,

Major-league Wonderful
Is someday going
To
Happen.

—Hafiz, "You're It"

In a compassionate
question, the focus
isn't on finding the
facts, drawing conclusions,
or making judgments; the
focus is on connection—
connection with the truth
of your story, connection
with the truth of your
soul, connection with
the truth of others, and
connection with the divine
within. Compassionate
questions move you closer
and closer to your whole
and holy self.

If I say "I am unbreakably yours" to one, I say it to all. I am unbreakably yours; I am unshakably yours. And now, you say it to me. It is a two-way street. I am your Beloved Guide, and you are my Beloved Guided. The Guide and the Guided. This is our partnership.

You have been invited to meet
The Friend.

No one can resist a Divine Invitation.
That narrows down all our choices
To just two:

We can come to God
Dressed for Dancing,
Or

Be carried on a stretcher
To God's Ward.

—Hafiz, "A Divine Invitation"

Ask knowing that the Voice hears and responds. Ask trusting that good is here—even if you can't see it yet. Ask knowing that you have already received. Ask knowing that you are a beloved child of a loving universe. Because that's what you are.

We know nothing until we know everything.
I have no object to defend
for all is of equal value
to me.

I cannot lose anything in this
place of abundance
I found.

—Saint Catherine, "This
Place of Abundance"

Give me everything mangled and bruised,
And I will make a light of it to make you weep,
and we will have rain
and begin again.

—Deena Metzger, "Leavings"

Every time you get to
a new place where
you realize something,
learn something,
know something, you
discover there's more
to explore, more to
uncover, more to learn.

Whenever you feel unsettled, go inside to that place of peace, fullness, well-being, and love. Reside there and center yourself in me. The externals are not reality and will pass. Rest in my peace, love, and joy. Trust me and trust in my divine timing. There is much to arrange. ever you feel unsettled, go inside to that place of peace, fullness, well-being, and love. Reside there and center yourself in me. The externals are not reality and will pass. Rest in my peace, love, and joy. Trust me and trust in my divine timing. There is much to arrange.

Don't surrender your loneliness
So quickly.
Let it cut more deep.

Let it ferment and season you
As few human
Or even divine ingredients can.
Something missing in my heart tonight,
Has made my eyes so soft,
My voice
So tender,

My need of God
Absolutely clear.

—Hafiz, "My Eyes So Soft"

It does seem that so
many experiences in life
happen with timing that
can only be described
as divinely guided.

There is nothing more perfect, nothing more important, than the authentic you.

I could tell you a priceless secret about
Your real worth, dear pilgrim,

But any unkindness to yourself,
Any confusion about others,

Will keep one
From accepting the grace, the love,

The sublime freedom
Divine knowledge always offers to you.

—Hafiz, "This Place Where You Are Right Now"

Give yourself permission
to want something more,
to expect something
more, to believe that you
deserve something more.

Your vision will become clear only when you look into your heart. Who looks outside, dreams. Who looks inside, awakens.

—Carl Jung

Blame

Keeps the sad game going.

—Hafiz, "The Sad Game"

As your soul shifts and changes in the course of writing down your soul, another person may well shift in a dancelike response, but don't write with the motivation of altering another person's behavior. Do it with the intention of deepening your understanding of yourself. Do it with the intention of exploring your own soul.

This is a romance.

Look
what happens to the scale
when love
holds
it.

It
stops
working.

—Kabir, "It Stops Working"

Dialogue with the Voice is a joyful, heart-lifting, soul-expanding adventure. It beckons only one response from our throats: Thank You!

A good gauge of spiritual
health is to write down
the three things you most want.
If they in any way differ,
you are in trouble.

—Rumi, "Spiritual Health"

Normal day, let me be aware of the treasure you are.
Let me learn from you, love you, bless you before you
depart. Let me not pass you by in quest of some rare
and perfect tomorrow. Let me hold you while I may,
for it may not always be so. One day I shall dig my
nails into the earth, or bury my face in the pillow,
or stretch myself taut, or raise my hands to the sky
and want, more than all the world, your return.

—Mary Jean Iron

The Voice meets you where you are, no matter what's happening in your life or what's working its way through your mind.

As soon as you opened your mouth
And I heard your soft
Sounds,

I knew we would be
Friends.
The first time, dear pilgrim, I heard
You laugh,

I knew it would not take me long
To turn you back into
God.

—Hafiz, "I Knew We Would Be Friends"

I've read all the books, but one
Only remains sacred: this
Volume of wonders, open
Always before my eyes.

—Kathleen Raine

Speak the Voice's
favorite language—the
Voice's only language:
the language of truth.

One cannot create one's next moment out of frustration with the present. Know that the moment before you is filled with beauty.

All your pain, worry, sorrow
Will someday apologize and confess
They were a great lie.

—Hafiz, "The Ear That Was Sold To a Fish"

Sometimes the light of clarification comes in the form of a klieg beam on the road not to take. All those things we call "bad luck" may actually be good guidance.

They can be like a sun, words.
They can do for the heart
what light can
for a field.

    —Saint John of the Cross, "They Can Be Like a Sun"

Your first thought is a precious gift. It is an impetus from deep within your soul that wants to be seen and heard. Honor it. Writing it down doesn't mean that it is true or has to happen. But it does mean that this thought is inside you and longs for expression.

You are about to embark on a very exciting, swift journey into realms and areas you don't know. You will feel unqualified, and yet, it is exactly your lack of qualifications in the worldly sense that make you ideal. We cheerfully and happily tell you to be open, to go with the flow, to follow your gut feelings and intuition, and savor every part of the journey.

Your joys and sufferings on this arduous path
Are lifting your worn veil lik

And will surely reveal your Magnificent Self.

—Hafiz, "They Call To You To Sing"

Explore the parts of yourself that stubbornly hold onto deeply ingrained, self-defeating thinking patterns.

My dear,
When anything ever touches or enters your body
Never say it is not Me—for God is just trying,
For the Beloved is just trying, to get close.

—Hafiz, "Never Say It Is Not Me"

The Voice is always present in the perfect, infinite, transcendent now. If you want to meet the Voice, be open and fully present in the now, and "that which wants to be heard" will make itself known.

Something has happened
To my understanding of existence
That now makes my heart always full of wonder
And kindness.

—Hafiz, "Today"

The truth is that we create ourselves by what we choose to notice, feel, think, say, and do. The operative word is "choose." Everything is a free will choice. Maybe we don't choose what happens, but we do choose how we react.

Now do you see?
Everything is sacred.
Everything is holy.

If God said,
"Rumi, pay homage to everything
that has helped you
enter my
arms,"

there would not be one experience of my life,
not one thought, not one feeling,
not any act, I
would not
bow
to.

—Rumi, "Rumi, Pay Homage"

Miracles are available
to anyone, any time.

Be kind to your sleeping heart.
Take it out into the vast fields of Light
And let it breathe.

Say,
"Love,
Give me back my wings.
Lift me,
Lift me nearer."

—Hafiz, "Awake Awhile"

Deep soul writing is not
something you have to do;
it's a gift you give yourself.

"We give thanks for all those times we have arisen from the depths or simply taken a tiny step toward something new."

—Molly Fumia

When you find yourself blurting out questions you've never asked before, questions that provoke you and possibly even scare you, be thankful.

Do not judge by your world's standards; judge by peace. When there is a sense of peace, you are on the right path.

"Be tough in the way a blade of grass is: rooted, willing to lean, and at peace with what is around it."

—Natalie Goldberg, *Wild Mind*

Complexity is a gift. Not knowing the right answers is a gift. Problems without apparent and immediate solutions are gifts.

Ask the Friend for love.
Ask Him again.

For I have learned that every heart will get
What it prays for
Most.

—Hafiz, "A Potted Plant"

Questions are a bridge
between where you are
and where you want to
be, what you know and
what you want to know,
who you are and who
you want to become.

A day of Silence
Can help you listen
To the Soul play
Its marvelous lute and drum.

—Hafiz, "Silence"

When you stop looking
for the answer, you start
getting answers—soul-
stirring, eye-popping,
life-changing answers.

There is nothing in your mind
You have not invited in.

There is no event in your life
You in some way
Did not drive a hard bargain for.

—Hafiz, "Practice This New Birdcall"

Mystical theta brain waves are the doorway between conscious mind and cosmic mind, self energy and source energy, old neural pathways and new neural pathways, life as it is and life as it could be. When we enter that mystical doorway, we walk into a new place.

I write of that journey
of becoming as
free as
God.

　　　　—Mirabai, "I Write of That Journey"

"The all-accepting
listener" is a perfect
description of the Voice.
And that perfect listener
awaits you every time
you pick up a pen.

I am unbreakably yours.

For

God

To make love,

For the divine alchemy to work,

The Pitcher needs a still cup.

Why

Ask Hafiz to say

Anything more about

Your most

Vital

Requirement?

—Hafiz, "A Still Cup"

The Voice can dish out
all the guidance in the
world, but your life
doesn't start changing
until you take action.

If your love letters are true dear God

I will surrender myself to

Who You keep saying

I

Am.

—Hafiz, "Without Brushing My Hair"

The ancient Africans taught that if a person is good to you, you must forever speak good of them. . . . In order to keep the good flowing, you must speak of it. . . . Everything we receive in life is food for our growth. If we eat from the plate, we must give thanks. Remembering, without that food, at the time, we may have starved.

—Ivanla Vanzant, *Acts of Faith*

The conversation happens all the time—not just in the moments you write.

Hope is the thing with feathers
That perches in the soul
And sings the tune without the words
And never stops—at all

—Emily Dickinson

The conversation never ends. It just continues and continues and continues until a day when you can no longer hold a pen, and then it continues in another place and in another way. The truth is, the conversation never ends. Isn't that divine?

There is something holy deep inside of you

That is so ardent and awake,

That needs to lie down naked

Next to God.

—Hafiz, "Among Strong Men"

The Voice already knows.
And because the Voice
already knows, you are
safe to tell the truth,
and, at the same time,
obligated to tell the truth.

This is the kind of Friend You are—

Without making me realize
My soul's anguished history,
You slip into my house at night,
And while I am sleeping,
You silently carry off
All my suffering and my sordid past
In Your beautiful
Hands.

— Hafiz, "Beautiful Hands"

It's what we all seek—someone to really, really listen.

Ever since Happiness heard your name,
It has been running through the streets
Trying to find you.

—Hafiz, "Several Times in the Last Week"

About the Author

Janet Conner is a popular writer and speaker with a simple message: We all have innate spiritual intelligence; we just need to know how to activate it. In her books, events, and worldwide courses, Janet shares practical spiritual tools that activate your divine Voice, engage your soul in vibrant dialogue, and magnify your creative potential.

Janet is the author of *Writing Down Your Soul* (Conari Press, 2008). Previously, she created *Spiritual Geography*, the soul writing system that heals the broken heart. Janet lives in Florida where she is exploring the ultimate question: What does your soul want? *Visit her at writingdownyoursoul.com.*

CPSIA information can be obtained
at www.ICGtesting.com
Printed in the USA
JSHW022102050121
10706JS00001B/1